A 1939 Sunbeam Talbot Ten at Wimbledon Common in January 1940. The bumper and running board edges are painted white to comply with black-out motoring regulations.

GW00357463

AUSTERITY MOTORING
1939-1950

Andrew Lane

Shire Publications Ltd

CONTENTS

Set in 9 point Times roman and printed in Great Britain by C. I. Thomas & Sons (Haverfordwest) Ltd, Press Buildings, Merlins Bridge, Haverfordwest, Dyfed.

Editorial Consultant: Michael E. Ware, Curator of the National Motor Museum, Beaulieu.

British Library Cataloguing in Publication Data available.

ACKNOWLEDGEMENTS
All the illustrations, including the front cover, are from the Photographic Library of the National Motor Museum, Beaulieu.

COVER: *A 1938 8 horsepower Morris in wartime trim.*

LEFT: *Many motorists laid their cars up for the duration of the war but this Renault 12 owner is getting ready to use his 6 gallons (27 litres) a month petrol ration for some Easter motoring in 1940.*

August 1939 in Dunster, Somerset, only days before the outbreak of war. In this idyllic scene can be seen an Austin Ruby and a Humber (right foreground). A Morris and a Wolseley are on the left.

WARTIME MOTORING

There was something special about August Bank Holiday, 1939. It seemed that all the cars in Britain, two million of them, were out on the roads. Everyone wanted to have a good time because the international news was so depressing. The motoring news that weekend was optimistic and confident — Cobb had just achieved a new land speed record of 368.85 mph (593.6 km/h), Sunbeam-Talbot announced their new 2 litre model and the Winchester bypass was nearly completed. The car trippers that weekend feared that this could be their last chance of pleasure motoring before the inevitable war began. They were right, and they would have been even more horrified had they realised that it would be eleven years before normality returned to motoring.

When Britain entered the Second World War on 3rd September 1939, the government already had detailed plans for motoring in wartime. Private motoring was not to be banned but on 23rd September petrol rationing came into effect. Those who tried to pre-empt the rationing by hoarding were taken to court and heavily fined. Petrol coupons were hastily issued in the first three weeks of war and varied according to the horsepower of the car. The ration was to provide for two hundred miles of motoring a month. Cars up to 7 horsepower were allowed 4 gallons (18.2 litres) a month, 8 and 9 horsepower cars, 5 gallons (22.7 litres), gradually rising to 10 gallons (45.5 litres) a month for cars of 20 horsepower and above. A motorist could have any kind of petrol so long as it was 'pool'. The petrol companies pooled their resources and it would be another fourteen years before their names glowed again at the pumps. In September 1939 pool petrol cost 1s 6d a gallon, rising to a wartime high of 2s 1½d in 1942. Where it could be found on the black market it cost 6s 6d a gallon. In an attempt to beat the black market, commercial fuel was dyed red but this could be rectified by filtering the fuel through a gas mask.

There were supplementary coupons available to those involved in essential work. In 1940 extra coupons could be obtained if a motorist volunteered to meet servicemen arriving late at a railway station to take them home. As well as the 'Get You Home' scheme there was also the 'Help Your Neighbour' scheme which encouraged drivers to carry a full load of passengers from the suburbs to the centre of London.

The measure which had the most immediate impact on motoring was the black-out. There had already been a practice night on 9th/10th August 1939 in central, southern and eastern England. In preparation for this, everything solid bordering a roadway was painted either completely white or with white stripes. Trees, lamp posts, kerbs, traffic lights, bollards and Belisha beacons all received the whitewash treatment. When war broke out it became compulsory for all car bumpers and the edges of running boards to be painted white. Then came the confusion over headlamp masks. The order was simple enough — all lights had to have blackened reflectors and a mask over one headlamp. The approved mask had one or several slits across it. The other headlamp had to have the bulb removed. The order did not say which headlamp had to be masked, so the motoring press and correspondence columns debated the advantages of masking either the offside or the nearside lamp. This was the period of the phoney war so

Mr Moore-Brabazon and his wife with their 1940 14 horsepower Vauxhall. For a brief period in 1941 Moore-Brabazon was Minister of Transport. Note the trees and bollards painted white for visibility in the black-out.

A large, seven-seater 1940 Humber Pullman limousine in service as a War Department staff car.

these issues seemed important. Rear and sidelights also had to be dimmed and two layers of newspaper were effective.

Driving in the black-out was a harrowing experience. Under the regulations, headlamps were meant to ensure that a car could be seen rather than to see with. Motorists were advised to dress warmly and have their windscreens opened up to improve visibility. Pedestrians were seen wearing white handkerchiefs attached to the fronts and backs of their coats, but this did not prevent the dreadful road accidents that occurred during the winter black-out months of 1939-40. In 1939 a total of 8,272 people were killed on the roads, a considerable increase on the 6,648 killed in 1938. In response to these accident figures a 20 mph (32 km/h) speed limit was imposed during the black-

out hours and in built-up areas from 1st February 1940. These measures failed to reduce the accident figures, which in 1941 rose to 9,200 deaths. The Army forbade men to hitch-hike after dark because it was too dangerous.

The process of advancing the clock one hour, known as Summer Time, was introduced for the first time on 25th February 1940 and increased to double Summer Time in 1941. This led to the memorable order: 'Summer Time will continue throughout the winter.'

During the summer of 1940 the phoney war ended and invasion became a real possibility. All road signs were removed, restricted areas around eastern and southern coasts were established and road blocks were set up. Any motorist failing to stop at a check point would be

An Austin Eight in a quiet Coventry back street in January 1940.

shot at. In addition, all car radios were banned and vehicles had to be immobilised when parked. It was recommended that the rotor arm or high tension leads should be removed or that the sparking plug leads should be crossed over. Although pleasure motoring was still permitted, many motorists decided it was not worthwhile and laid up their cars until the end of the war.

The Motor was quick to point out that this was not in the national interest. 'Love of country is, in war, a necessity as well as a virtue. Nevertheless those who think that cutting down their tax contribution by, say, £30 per annum, helping to ruin their local garage man, reducing to bare paper value the £150 million invested in a retail motor business, adding to the burden of public transport and, incidentally, denying themselves health and pleasure, is a course well

calculated to assist our war effort, are deceiving themselves'.

Thousands of private cars were put to use as part of the war effort on the home front. In return for their services drivers could claim supplementary petrol coupons. Owners volunteered their cars for a wide variety of uses — providing lifts for servicemen and the elderly, for hospital visits, distributing goods and taking evacuee children to their new homes. The WVS (Women's Voluntary Service) made a vital contribution in this area. Volunteers were asked, 'Do you mind a young child being sick in the back of your car?' In the crisis summer months of 1940, fourteen thousand vehicles were mobilised for ambulance purposes with the ARP and a further fifteen thousand cars were on standby to carry sitting wounded.

The issue of pleasure motoring became

ABOVE: *A blitzed 1934 Morris-Commercial taxicab. The taxi business in London was severely curtailed because over a third of the fleet was requisitioned for war work, petrol was rationed to 3 gallons (13.6 litres) a day and illuminated meter signs were forbidden in the black-out.*
BELOW: *Staff cars were needed in huge numbers by the armed forces. These Vauxhall Fourteens have been reconditioned for the RAF. The petrol globes still carry brand names even though they dispensed only 'pool' petrol.*

Gas was the main alternative fuel to pertrol in wartime London. Producer gas trailers (left) were used by buses, trucks and cars. The car-roof gas bag (right) was unwieldy at speed or in a strong wind.

a subject of fierce public debate. The sight of a packed car park at the Derby stirred many to call motorists unpatriotic and press articles asked motorists to choose between 'joy rides or victory marches? Pleasure now or slavery for a lifetime.' An MP went further: 'Every gallon of petrol used in this country is mixed with the blood of seamen.' *The Motor* countered the argument by providing statistics that showed that only three tankers a month, out of a fleet of two thousand at sea, were needed to provide the basic ration for motorists. The debate ended in July 1942 when the basic ration was withdrawn altogether and only those who could prove their journeys were essential were allowed petrol. Essential journeys could include going shopping (for those in rural areas), hospital visits, attending church or taking children to school. With the fall of Singapore and Malaya in February 1942 new regulations on tyres were rushed in. Only those with 'E' (essential) petrol coupons could have tyres and they had to apply in writing to the Divisional Petroleum Officer. It became illegal for a private owner to dispose of his tyres only. If the tyres were transferred to someone else the car had to go with them.

Alternative fuels made a limited comeback into motoring. The most common alternative to petrol was gas which was available in two forms. Firstly, there was the low pressure gas stored in bags attached to the car roof or carried in a trailer. A visit to the town gasworks for a fill-up would cost 1s 9d and was required after 20 - 30 miles (32-48 km), depending on the efficiency of the car. By the end of 1942 there were about a thousand private cars with gas bags but the idea never became popular because of the numerous disadvantages: for instance, the bag flapped about and made the car unstable, range was limited and gas supplies were available only in the London area. Another form of supply was a gas producer. The contrivance was fixed to the back of a car or on a trailer and used coal, coke or wood as fuel. The Ennis gas producer cost £65 and gave a 80 mile (113 - 129 km) range before refilling. However, there was a loss of 40 to 50 per cent of power and most motorists preferred to stay with (or without) a petrol ration rather than pay conversion costs.

THE MOTOR INDUSTRY

Car production did not instantly cease when war began in September 1939. In early 1940 there were still on average 3,500 new registrations a month and there were still 130 models available. The car manufacturers were instructed by the government to continue production for the export market. There was no rush of government orders for military vehicles, but then this was the phoney war. The shock of war was to come later. So from October 1939 to May 1940 an average of five thousand cars a month was exported, with Austin alone producing ten thousand cars for export in that period. Ford even announced a new model in 1940, the Anglia, but production was short-lived.

In July 1940 the government took over the stocks of all new and unregistered cars for disposal abroad and banned the purchase of an unregistered car except by special licence. A year later the government allowed the limited production of new cars for private motorists on essential work, so in July 1941 Austin, Morris, Ford and Hillman were all producing 8 and 10 horsepower cars which had the added cost of the recently introduced purchase tax.

The enormous production potential of the motor industry in wartime had been examined prior to 1939. The 'Shadow Factory' scheme of 1936 planned for the leading motor manufacturers to mass-produce aircraft in the event of war. To cope with this situation additional factories were built near the parent companies. During the war Ford, Nuffield, Austin

Gas producers could burn coal, coke or wood but they were never popular. The costs of equipment and conversion in return for a sluggish engine performance made gas producers generally unattractive to private motorists.

During the war Austin, Hillman, Morris and Standard made pick-up vans on pre-war passenger car chassis. This is a 1940 Standard 12 horsepower light utility van with the distinctive simple wire-mesh radiator grille.

and Daimler produced huge quantities of aircraft and aero engines like the Rolls-Royce Merlin and Bristol Mercury. Volume car production ceased and workers found themselves producing a wide variety of war material such as torpedos, mines, trucks, armoured cars, bren gun carriers, jerricans, rocket launchers, munitions, Bailey bridges, gliders and, vitally, tanks.

For the workers hours were long and holidays rare. Even Boxing Day ceased to be a bank holiday. The car plants at Coventry, Birmingham, Oxford and Dagenham were prime targets during the blitz. In just one attack on Coventry, on 14th November 1940, at least 130 of 180 principal factories were damaged. With twenty thousand houses also rendered uninhabitable, this destruction became known as 'Coventration'.

As the war entered its final phase from autumn 1944 thoughts were turned to the reconstruction of post-war Britain. Fanciful dreams for the motorist would include the rapid end of petrol rationing, plenty of new cars for everyone again, and, perhaps, even a British 'people's car'. All the roads would be improved, with a new sign system and, best of all, motorways would span the country just like autobahns. In 1939 the County Surveyors Society had published a plan for 1000 miles (1600 km) of motorways. The Minister of Transport, Mr Barnes, announced in March 1946 that a motorway would be built from South Wales to the Midlands but it was to be 1959 before the first motorway was opened in Britain. It was going to take longer to achieve the reconstruction dreams than most people realised and the needs of the motorist were low on the list of government priorities.

This scene of Cook Street car park, Liverpool, in 1946 amply illustrates how 1930s cars were the only ones available in the immediate post-war years. Fords, Morrises, Vauxhalls, Austins and an MG can all be seen on this flattened bomb site.

PEACETIME AUSTERITY

The major motor manufacturers had been so engrossed in the war effort that when peace came they had no new car designs to offer. The priority was to produce cars again as part of the economic recovery programme. The cost of retooling was prohibitive so the 1940 machinery resumed production of 1940 models.

Austin returned to producing cars in August 1945 with their 8, 10 and 12 horsepower saloons. A new 16 horsepower model was introduced which was basically the same as a 12 but with a 2199 cc overhead-valve engine instead of a 1535 cc side-valve unit. Ford returned with the 8 horsepower Anglia, introduced at the start of the war, and the 10 horsepower Prefect. The Anglia, with its 933 cc four-cylinder side-valve engine, remained unchanged until 1948. In August 1946 a Prefect became the millionth

vehicle to emerge from the Dagenham plant. The Morris range for 1946 comprised the pre-war series E Eight and series M Ten.

Despite the predominance of reintroduced 1940 models, some companies had anticipated the return to car production by producing new designs during the war or working up models planned for 1940-1. Armstrong-Siddeley introduced their post-war models in May 1945 during the same week as VE Day. The 16 horsepower Lanchester saloon and Hurricane drophead coupé were joined by the Typhoon two-door saloon in August 1946. The famous fighter aircraft names indicated the type of military production Armstrong-Siddeley had been undertaking during the war. The Bristol Aeroplane Company went into quantity production of the Bristol 400 in 1947. The 1971 cc overhead-valve engine with three

11

ABOVE: *When Morris resumed car production in 1945 they reintroduced their 1939-40 Eight and Ten saloons. This 1947 series M Morris Ten four-door saloon differed from the 1939 model by having a restyled curved radiator grille to replace the previous flat pattern.*

BELOW: *The Ford Anglia E04A first appeared in 1940, which was not an auspicious time to launch a new model. Made until 1948, the Anglia was essentially the 1938 8 horsepower model in more modern styling. In all, nearly 59,000 were made.*

SU carburettors was a direct copy of the BMW 328. As one would expect from an aircraft company, the body was beautifully streamlined and based on extensive wind-tunnel testing.

In September 1945 Riley brought out an entirely new and elegant 1½ litre model. The engine was of pre-war design but new features were a totally new bodywork and independent front suspension. In the following year a 2½ litre model was introduced. Triumph had been taken over by Standard in 1944 but two entirely new Triumph cars were announced in 1945. The 1800 series 18 T Saloon and series 18 TR Roadster each had a 1776 cc four-cylinder overhead-valve engine, but their styling was very different. The Saloon had the 'razor edge' design while the Roadster featured long, low lines and curved rear end. Triumph was the first British company to introduce column gear change.

Anyone who dreamed that after VE Day in May 1945 motoring would return to the rosy 1939 days was to be disillusioned. On 1st June the basic petrol ration was restored but only at 5 gallons (23 litres) a month for 10 horsepower cars, which was less than the September 1939 ration. There was to be no return to a free market for cars because licences giving permission to buy a car were to be issued only if the use was essential. Car production resumed but immediately the government said 50 per cent had to be exported. Materials were in short supply so production was modest.

Rocketing car prices became a feature of post-war motoring. In September 1939 an Austin Ten cost £175 but in November 1947 it was £435; a Rover Sixteen had risen from £360 to £942. A major inflationary factor was the 33⅓ per cent purchase tax, introduced in 1940. Cars over £1000 carried 66⅔ per cent

Sidney Allard, a well known pre-war trials competitor, began his own quantity production of Allard cars in 1946. The L-Type open four-seater had independent front suspension, lightweight chassis and a developed version of the Ford V8 3.6 litre engine.

13

OT **11156**   This Book is the property of His Majesty's Government   )T **11156**

Motor Fuel Ration Book

FOR THE SIX MONTHS

SEPTEMBER, 1946 to FEBRUARY, 1947

Private Motor Car

Registered No. of Vehicle

K N /.

Date and Office of Issue

ued under the authority of the FUEL and POWER

THREE UNITS

20 H.P. AND OVER

The coupons in this book authorise the furnishing and acquisition of the number of units of motor fuel specified on the coupons.
The issue of a ration book does not guarantee to the holder any minimum quantity of motor fuel and the coupons contained in this book may be cancelled at any time.
Any person furnishing or acquiring motor fuel otherwise than in accordance with the provisions of the Order for the time being in force under which these coupons are issued or contrary to the conditions appearing thereon will be liable to prosecution.

WT. 9208 44-245

coupon is
ALID
month of
RY, 1947

S DRAWN TO THE
AND CONDITIONS
NG OVERLEAF

Petrol ration coupons were swiftly introduced in September 1939 and remained a part of everyday motoring until May 1950. In the period of this coupon (September 1946 to February 1947) a 20 horsepower car was entitled to 15 gallons (68 litres) a month.

purchase tax. The lack of new cars caused a boom period for the second-hand car market. It was a sellers' market with prices continually increasing. A random glance through the classified advertisements in 1948 reveals a 1932 Austin Ten for sale at 310 guineas, twice its purchase price sixteen years earlier. Second hand cars were costing more than new ones. A two-year-old 1½ litre Riley, for example, sold for £950 yet it was only £863 new, and a 1946 Morris Ten, originally £423, was £595 second-hand. In an effort to prevent profiteers ordering several new cars and then selling them immediately at inflated prices, the British Motor Trade Association introduced a covenant scheme in July 1946. Under this scheme a buyer had to guarantee to keep his new car for a minimum of six months and from March 1947 the period became twelve months.

An agreement document had to be signed and strictly adhered to. The scheme proved very successful and since the demand for cars was still very high in 1950 the period was extended to two years.

1947 was a grim year for everyone. The tough austerity measures of Sir Stafford Cripps, Chancellor of the Exchequer in the Labour government, made life very dull. 1947 was dominated by the worsening economic situation. Britain was on the verge of bankruptcy, a consequence of the war and because imports were rising well above exports. The situation became critical and the government's repeated message to industry was to export.

The motor industry was told to 'export or die'. The government raised the export quota of the motor industry to 75 per cent and still supplies were only

ABOVE: *Introduced in 1939, pool petrol continued in use until 1953 when brand names finally returned. Filling up is a Triumph Renown.*

BELOW: *A 1949 Austin A90 Atlantic convertible being correctly filled with pool petrol for private vehicles only. Anyone found with red-dyed commercial fuel in their tank faced severe penalties. The A90 was unashamedly American in design and fast, with a top speed of 95 mph (153 km/h).*

15

ABOVE: *A fleet of MG TCs bought by the Kent police force in 1946. The TC, basically the same as the 1939 TB, had a 1250 cc four-cylinder engine and was produced from 1945 to 1949. The majority were exported to North America.*
BELOW: *Donald Healey began producing cars in 1946 at the rate of five a week. The 1946 Roadster, like the saloon, used a Riley-based 2.4 litre engine and could reach 100 mph (161 km/h). The headlamps were concealed beneath flaps which rose when the lamps were turned on.*

ABOVE: *By 1948 75 per cent of all cars were exported. This picture shows Manchester Docks when 420 Austin A40s were sent in one shipment to the United States and Canada.*
BELOW: *The 1948 Rover P3 series featured two models, the Sixty with four cylinders and the Seventy-five with six cylinders. This 1949 Seventy-five, although similar to the previous Twelve, featured a new engine (2103 cc) with overhead inlet and side exhaust valves.*

available on condition that production targets were met. As 1947 began the industry was already straining under the added restriction of major shortages of coal, copper, leather, sheet steel and manpower. The bleak economic outlook was compounded by the weather as the hardest winter on record hit Britain. The country was gripped by Arctic conditions for weeks on end. In February the weather was a contributory cause of a massive coal shortage which led to the shutdown of all major industries, car manufacturing included. It was a severe blow and Sir Miles Thomas of the Nuffield Organisation said: 'At a conservative estimate, over 10 per cent of the year's potential output from the whole industry has been lost.' For the private motorist 1947 was the bleakest year ever. The winter conditions curtailed use of the meagre basic petrol ration and the increased export drive meant that the chances of buying a new car were ever more remote. There was sympathetic understanding of the car shortage as most people were aware of the economic crisis and believed that everyone should pull together. However, petrol rationing was slightly different. The government's argument on the need for rationing (because petrol was purchased in dollars) became less and less convincing. Motorists asked why, if dollars were in short supply, was there no restriction on the £30 million spent on tobacco imports and the £19 million spent on American films?

The final straw came on 27th August when the government announced that even the basic ration was to be removed, as it had been in 1942, but the situation now was entirely different. The government's claim that £5 million would be saved was scorned as absurd in relation to the £600 million deficit. The outcry against the abolition of the basic ration was widespread. *The Autocar* com-

The Riley 2½ litre RMB series saloon was one of the first new post-war designs. Based on a pre-war Riley Sixteen, the chassis was entirely new and with stylish bodywork. The 2½ litre had the distinctive pale blue radiator badge, while the 1½ litre's badge was dark blue.

The Jowett Javelin was first announced in 1946 and went into production the following year. This totally new design had a horizontally opposed 1486 cc four-cylinder overhead-valve engine mounted ahead of the front axle. Column gear change and the enveloping bodywork reflected the influence of American design.

mented: 'The abolition of a basic ration is savage, it involves more hardship, financial loss and deprivation than any comparable act, and it savours strongly of class discrimination.' The AA presented a petition of one million signatures to the House of Commons. *The Times* recorded that 'The government now know that no restriction has been more unpopular'. The basic ration was eventually restored in June 1948 but at a further reduced rate of one third of the old basic, that is, only 90 miles a month (145 km). The allowance would not allow a London motorist to go to Brighton and back once a month, although he might manage Southend.

Along with the restoration of the ration came the Motor Spirit (Regulation) Act, the so-called Red Petrol Act, aimed at the black market. In future petrol pumps could only dispense two kinds of petrol, either red for commercial vehicles or yellow for private cars. Any private motorist found with red petrol in his tank

would face the severe penalties of having his driving licence suspended and a fine of up to £1000 and imprisonment. A garage owner dispensing incorrect fuel would have his retail petrol supply business suspended. This law became very unpopular and the chairman of a bench of Welsh magistrates was dismissed after he said: 'We dislike the wording of this Act intensely. We do not call it British — we call it a very evilly worded Act.' *The Autocar* wrote, 'The heavy hand of totalitarianism has taken a step forward.' The antipathy to the act was heightened when it was revealed that official government cars all used red petrol with the full approval of the Ministry of Supply.

The full impact of the shortages in fuel and cars was shown when an AA traffic census in 1948 revealed that road traffic was only half what it had been in 1937. The progress of the motor car, which had been so rapid prior to 1937, seemed to have been arrested for the past ten years.

ABOVE: *Only three months after VJ Day Armstrong-Siddeley were back in production with a new car, the Hurricane drophead coupé. Described as 'cars with aircraft quality', the Armstrong-Siddeley Hurricane is pictured taking part in the 1952 London Rally.*

BELOW: *The sleek and elegant Bristol 401 alongside the giant Bristol Brabazon at Filton. The 400 series used 2 litre, six-cylinder engines developed from the pre-war BMW 328 and capable of 90 mph (145 km/h).*

ABOVE: *Eastgate Street, Gloucester, in August 1947 shows relatively few private cars in use. On the left is a 1929 Riley, a pre-war Commer truck, and a Hillman Minx in RAF service. On the right are a series E Morris 8, a Vauxhall 12 and an Austin Cambridge.*
BELOW: *Sir John Black of the Standard Motor Company seated on the new Vanguard in 1947. Production began in 1948 but for export only. The Vanguard was a totally new design with a 2088 cc, four-cylinder overhead-valve engine, independent front suspension, three-speed gearbox and column gear change.*

The Daimler stand at the 1948 Earls Court Motor Show. In the foreground (left) is the 2½ litre, four-door saloon model. Next to it is the 2½ litre DB18 Special Sports coupé. Note the other company banners around the hall with names that have long gone.

THE 1948 MOTOR SHOW

Britain had been deprived of a Motor Show since 1938. Now, ten years on, the car-hungry public were seized with excitement and anticipation. There had been a few new models introduced since the war but it was known that many manufacturers were going to use the Motor Show for their long-awaited new cars. The Motor Show opened at Earls Court in October and *The Autocar* editorial ran: 'The dark decade of the war and post-war period has gone; the new cars radiate a heartening gleam. They may well prove to be the light at the end of the gloom-ridden road along which motoring has travelled over the past ten years'. However, to prepare the show visitors for what they were about to see, came this warning: 'The car at Earls Court — and

British motorists must face the fact squarely — is designed more for the foreign customer than for the motorist at home. It will have more flashiness about it than many British motorists would like but it is a flashiness that will look well, and go down well, in places like Port Said'.

Twenty-one entirely new models were launched at the Motor Show. The greatest attractions were the Jaguar XK 120 and Mark V Saloon, the Morris Minor and the Standard Vanguard. To the press and public they were sensational. In addition to these cars the following also made their debut: the Aston Martin DB1, Austin A70/A90, Bristol 402, Frazer-Nash, Hillman Minx, Humber Hawk, Lagonda 2½ litre, Morris Oxford and

22

ABOVE: *Clark Gable in an XK120 in 1950. The debut of the Jaguar XK engine was undoubtedly the sensation of 1948. It was the power behind the XK120. Sleek and aerodynamic in design, capable of 120 mph (193 km/h), it cost only £1273. No XK120s were sold in Britain before March 1950.*

BELOW: *The XK engine was not available on Jaguar saloons until 1951 so the 1948 Jaguar range consisted of earlier Sixes with a facelift and called the Mark V series. New features included independent front suspension and sloping windscreens. This is the the 1948 3½ litre drophead coupé.*

ABOVE: *The Morris Minor, destined to become one of Britain's most popular cars, made its first appearance at the 1948 Motor Show. Designed by Alec Issigonis, it had bulbous styling, excellent steering qualities and independent front suspension. The ageing 8 horsepower unit was used at first but replaced in 1952 with the Austin 803 cc A type engine.*

BELOW: *The Hillman stand for their Mark III Minx at the first post-war Motor Shows was spectacular. The Minx had been restyled several times since it first appeared in 1931. The Mark III cost £505.*

Six, Rover P3, Singer SM 1500, Sunbeam Talbot 80 and 90, Vauxhall Wyvern and Velox, Wolseley 4/50 and 6/80. The visitors were staggered by the advances made in independent front suspension, which was now commonplace, and the smooth shape of the cars. Lamps, door handles and running boards were now merged into the bodywork. It was a completely new look and the American influence was evident throughout.

Even if the British public could not buy the cars because of the export priority, they wanted to see them and, with foreign visitors, the attendance at the show was a record 563,000. The introduction of so many new models made the 1948 show a classic.

THE NEW CAR DESIGNS

The 1948 Motor Show revealed to the public for the first time the major directions in which car design was heading. Since there had been no motor show for ten years the surprise was all the greater. The designers were reacting to sudden new outside influences on their products.

The export trade, the new vehicle taxation system, American styling advances and new technologies learnt from the wartime production of aircraft all had a profound effect on the design of cars in the late 1940s.

In 1939 only some seven British cars in a hundred were exported, therefore British cars were designed wholly with British needs in mind. Those needs were fulfilled by a car which ran at moderate speeds over narrow, crowded but well surfaced roads and which could rely on the tight network of garages and repair shops all over Britain. In 1945 when car production resumed, the market was completely reversed; the 1939 car had suddenly to become a world car. The foreign market required cars which could cope with long, straight roads with bumpy surfaces which made engine reliability and low fuel consumption at full throttle a priority. Mountain passes with ascents and descents of 15 miles (24 km) made steering, cornering and brakes of vital importance. Constant high speeds in hot countries made cooling another priority.

In July 1948 Vauxhall replaced their Twelve and Fourteen saloons with the Wyvern and Velox models. The Velox, shown here, had a 2275 cc six-cylinder engine compared to the weaker Wyvern's four-cylinder 1442 cc unit. In 1949 the Velox was priced at £550.

A sleek Lea Francis 14 horsepower, two-seater sports model. This was introduced in 1948 to join the existing Lea Francis range of the Fourteen saloon, coupé and utility models.

By the winter of 1947-8 the British motor industry was receiving a flood of service complaints from all over the world. The industry could not understand why their highly reputed cars were falling to pieces or breaking down so often until they discovered the conditions in which the cars were used and for which they had certainly not been designed. So by 1947, when the export quota was 75 per cent with no signs of diminishing, car design was being completely rethought to meet the demands of the foreign buyer. The export trade was not the sole reason for the adoption of independent front suspension, but it was an important contributory factor. The rigid front axle and leaf springs of the 1939 models constituted a major weakness and all true post-war designs featured independent

It was easier to buy a new British car abroad than it was in Britain. This scene shows a Vauxhall Fourteen on a well made road in Sierra Leone in 1948. Generally British cars suffered badly on foreign roads and in climates they were not designed for.

26

In March 1947 at the Geneva Salon Austin unveiled two entirely new six-cylinder models, the A110 Sheerline and the A120 Princess (A120 prototype shown). The Princess used a 3½ litre truck engine and triple SU carburretors and its coachwork was by Vanden Plas.

front suspension. There had been considerable problems with this system, particularly with wear, but now there were fewer moving parts and steering and suspension joints were better designed. By the 1949 Motor Show independent front suspension was virtually universal.

The radical changes were in body styling and interior features. The foreign buyers' taste for modern looks and the American advances in style were the main influences here. The trend in the late 1940s was for full-width, fully enveloping bodywork with submerged headlamps. The smooth form was not an overnight transition and at the 1948 Motor Show there were some ugly compromises. The bulbous look was pure 1942 American styling and so were the other imports, of bench seats for three at

A 1948 Triumph 1800 Roadster, series 18TR. The roadster was introduced in 1946 with a saloon model. From October 1948 it was fitted with a Standard Vanguard engine and renamed the 2000 Roadster, Series 20TR.

27

The once illustrious Lagonda company was ailing by 1947 but was saved by David Brown of Aston Martin. He reintroduced the 2.6 litre Lagonda in 1948 but at a price of £3100, including 66⅔ per cent purchase tax, it is not surprising that only 520 were sold.

the front and column gear change. Triumph had pioneered the use of the new gear position in 1946 but by 1948 it was finding far wider acceptance and could be found on Austin, Hillman, Humber, Jowett, Morris, Singer, Standard, Triumph, Vauxhall and Wolseley models.

The sliding roof was a fast disappearing feature in 1948 because it was totally unsuitable for foreign conditions such as monsoons in the Far East or dust in Africa. Keeping dust out of cars became a serious problem for British designers. The advance of air conditioning and heating as standard features in cars was attributable to the demands of the export market.

The British motorist still considered these features as luxuries unlike the

The Triumph Mayflower with its razor-edged styling caused a sensation when it first appeared in September 1949. The public either loved or hated its looks. The Mayflower used a 1247 cc side-valve engine.

buyer from Sweden or Egypt who thought of them as vital. Therefore at the 1948 Motor Show fifteen makes had heaters as standard and the majority had them as optional extras.

Engine development was greatly assisted in 1945 by the removal of the car tax based on the 'RAC rating'. Since 1920 cars had been taxed according to horsepower, which was calculated by piston area rather than by the stroke and therefore the cubic capacity. This led to most British cars having long-stroke, small bore engines with the resulting poor power output and efficiency. The horsepower rating was a deterrent to progress so to boost exports the govern-ment abandoned the system. For 1947 a new taxation scheme came into opera-tion. The tax would be £1 per 100 cc of engine size, which meant £10 for a Ford Anglia but £41 for a Humber Super Snipe. The cc tax was very unpopular for being unfair so in 1948 Hugh Dalton brought in the flat-rate tax of £10 per car. After twenty-eight years the restrictive taxes on engine sizes were gone and manufacturers became free to build the engines they and their customers wanted. *The Autocar* commented that the new flat-rate tax 'will ultimately prove to have caused a revolution in the British motor industry'.

THE BEGINNING OF THE END

There were signs in 1950 that this year was going to be the beginning of the end of austerity. Rationing was gradually ending with clothes and then soap being released in 1949 and 1950. Petrol restrictions were still a major controversy and when rationing ended in Germany before it did in Britain this was denounced as the last straw. Petrol rationing finally ended in Britain on 26th May 1950.

It was still very difficult to obtain a new car and the pressure on companies to export remained just as strong. However, many new and exciting models appeared to keep the car-starved public flocking to the 1949 and 1950 Motor Shows. The outstanding models for 1949 were the Rover 75 P4 series and the Triumph Mayflower. The Rover was more of a redesign whereas the Mayflower was an entirely new model.

In complete contrast to the 'razor edge' styling of the Mayflower was the Austin A90 Atlantic convertible, a direct copy of current American styling. Austin, a company not known for high performance cars, suddenly produced a sleek 95 mph (153 km/h) car with lively acceleration. The A90 was designed specifically for the American market and consequently fea-tured as standard such gadgets as power-operated hood and windows and winking indicators. The *Autocar* road test of 1949 described the A90 as 'one of the select band of "star" cars produced since the war, of outstanding merit and appeal'.

By the end of the 1940s most manufac-turers had produced their new post-war ranges which were to take them into the mid 1950s and beyond. After a decade of stagnation, motor car development was moving forward again. However, it was not until the 1950 Motor Show that Ford unveiled their new-look cars. The Consul had a 1508 cc four-cylinder unit, while the Zephyr used a six-cylinder 2262 cc engine. This was the first time Ford had built a Six in Britain. The Consul sold at a basic price of £415 and the Zephyr for £475.

Other new models announced in 1950 included the Aston Martin DB2, the Jowett Jupiter, the Austin A70 Hereford saloon and coupé and the Morgan Plus Four. However the sensation of the year was the Jaguar Mark VII in which, for the first time, the XK engine powered a full-size saloon.

The 1950 Motor Show had an array of styles that implied anything but austerity. New cars were in production and petrol rationing had gone, and motoring was returning to normal.

ABOVE: *AC Cars Limited introduced the 2 litre saloon in 1947 and it remained in production until 1956. The 1991 cc overhead-camshaft engine had three SU carburettors and an output of 74 brake horsepower. A drophead coupé version was briefly produced in 1949.*

BELOW: *In October 1950 Ford unveiled their long awaited new car styles. The Consul (left) had the new four-cylinder 1.5 litre overhead-valve engine. The Zephyr had the equally new six-cylinder 2.3 overhead-value engine.*

ABOVE: *A strange sight. A 1947-8 Alvis TA14 with a Caffyn Estate body reminiscent of the American style of wooden-bodied shooting brakes. Alvis produced the TA14 in chassis and complete saloon form from 1946 to 1950.*

BELOW: *In 1950 Jowett developed their successful Javelin into the more powerful Jupiter of which this is the prototype. The Jupiter used a flat four, 1486 cc engine with a 60 brake horsepower output. With an alluminium body and aerodynamic styling the Jupiter could cruise easily at 80 mph (129 km/h).*

FURTHER READING

Fairfax, Ernest. *Calling All Arms.* Hutchinson, 1945.
Graves, Charles. *Drive for Freedom.* Hodder and Stoughton, 1944.
Olyslager Auto Library. *British Cars of the Early Forties.* Warne, 1974.
Olyslager Auto Library. *British Cars of the Late Forties.* Warne, 1974.
Robson, Graham. *The Post War Touring Car.* Haynes, 1977.
Sedgwick, Michael. *Cars of the Thirties and Forties.* Hamlyn, 1979.
Sedgwick, Michael. *The Motor Car 1946-56.* Batsford, 1979.
Lukins, A. *British Motor Cars 1950/51.* George Ronald, 1950.

PLACES TO VISIT

Birmingham Museum of Science and Industry, Newhall Street, Birmingham B3 1RZ. Telephone: 021-236 1022.
Britain in the Blitz, Cornwall Aero Park and Flambards Victorian Village, Culdrose Manor, Helston, Cornwall TR13 0GA. Telephone: Helston (0326) 574549 or 573404.
British Motor Industry Heritage Trust, Heritage Collection, Syon Park, Brentford, Middlesex TW8 3JF. Telephone: 01-560 1378.
Campden Car Collection, High Street, Chipping Campden, Gloucestershire GL55 6HB. Telephone: Broadway (0386) 840289.
Museum of Army Transport, Flemingate, Beverley, North Humberside HU17 0NG. Telephone: Hull (0482) 860445.
National Motor Museum, John Montagu Building, Beaulieu, Brockenhurst, Hampshire SO4 7ZN. Telephone: Beaulieu (0590) 612345.

This gathering in north Devon in 1951 illustrates clearly the changing face of car design and how 1930s cars still featured largely in the motoring scene. A 1949 Morris Minor, 1934 Rover 10/12, 1950 Vauxhall Wyvern and a 1931 Austin 7 are just some of many cars present.